A is for Alberta

for

by Mindy Johnstone

A IS FOR ALBERTA

Published by

Summerthought

Summerthought Publishing
PO Box 2309
Banff, AB T1L 1C1
Canada
www.summerthought.com

Layout: Linda Petras
Printed and bound in Canada by Friesens

We gratefully acknowledge the financial support of the Government of Alberta through the Alberta Media Fund
and the Government of Canada through the Canada Book Fund for our publishing activities.

Library and Archives Canada Cataloguing in Publication

Title: A is for Alberta / by Mindy Johnstone.

Names: Johnstone, Mindy, author, illustrator.

Identifiers: Canadiana 20220427577 | ISBN 9781926983554 (hardcover)

Subjects: LCSH: English language—Alphabet—Juvenile literature. | LCSH: Alberta—Juvenile literature.
| LCGFT: Alphabet books.

Classification: LCC PE1155 .J66 2022 | DDC j421/.1—dc23

A $^{is}_{for}$ Alberta

by Mindy Johnstone

A is for Alberta,
our province out West

B is for Banff,
where bears like to rest

C is for coulee and cattle galore

D is for Drumheller — oh look, a dinosaur!

E is for Edmonton,
with big city parks

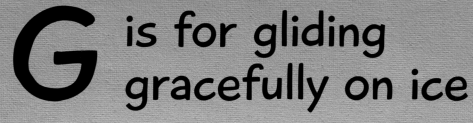

G is for gliding
gracefully on ice

H is for hot springs that feel really nice

J is for Jasper and jumping in lakes

K is for kettle, kindling and knots

L is for lasso, lanterns and logs

M is for a magpie that lands anywhere

N is for northern lights,
dancing in the air

O
is for owl,
Alberta's
Great
Horned

P

is for
paddling
on a
crisp
summer
morn

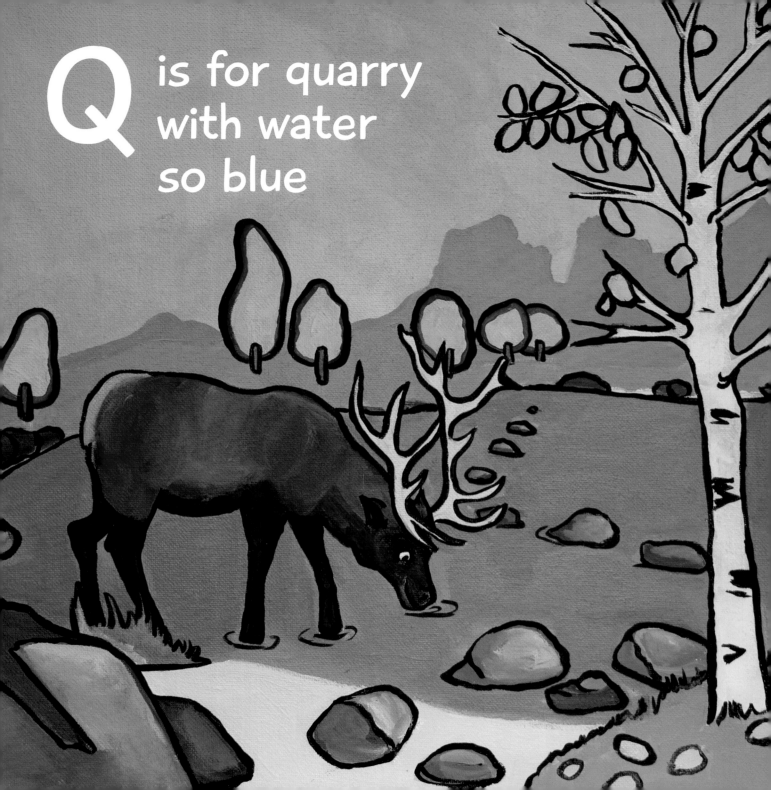

Q is for quarry
with water
so blue

R is for railroad —
Choo! Choo!

S is for Stampede,
the greatest outdoor show

T is for tractors and trailers they tow

U is for

Up! Up! Up!
and away

V is for valleys
where we like to play

Discover fun facts about Alberta from A to Z

 **A:** Riding a horse is a traditional form of transportation in Alberta.

 **E:** Edmonton, Alberta's capital, is known as "The Festival City."

 **B:** Dating to 1885, Banff is Canada's oldest national park.

 **F:** Head to Red Rock Canyon in Waterton Lakes National Park to see fossils from ancient sea beds.

 **C:** Coulees are valleys eroded by ancient rivers.

 **G:** Each winter, Lake Louise hosts an ice-carving competition.

 **D:** Visit the museum at Drumheller to see why this region is the Dinosaur Capital of the World.

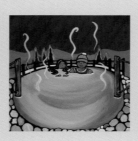 **H:** Miette Hot Springs is the hottest natural pool in the Canadian Rockies.

I: Ice fishing at Sylvan Lake is a popular winter sport.

L: Search out the traditions of Alberta's pioneers at local ranches.

O: The great horned owl is Alberta's official bird.

J: Horseshoe Lake in Jasper National Park is where swimmers jump for joy.

M: Magpies and elk are common in mountain towns.

P: At over 1,000 kilometres, imagine how long it would take to paddle the Peace River in a canoe!

K: Camp cooking is a great way to enjoy local food.

N: Wood Buffalo National Park is an ideal place to view the northern lights.

Q: Quarry Lake, in the town of Canmore, is a great spot to cool off on a hot summer's day.

R: Trains deliver Alberta's crops across the country.

U: Bighorn sheep are common throughout the Canadian Rockies.

X: The town of Vulcan is known as the Star Trek Capital of Canada. It's out of this world!

S: The Calgary Stampede is the "Greatest Outdoor Show on Earth."

V: In winter, Albertans of all ages can be found tobogganing and skiing.

Y: The white cowboy hat is a symbol of welcome in Calgary.

T: Alberta's vast prairies grow large crops of wheat and barley.

W: Alberta has two major hockey teams, the Edmonton Oilers and the Calgary Flames.

Z: One of the best ways to experience Alberta is to camp in wide open spaces.